٢

Put Beginning Readers on the Right Track with ALL ABOARD READING™

The All Aboard Reading series is especially for beginning readers. Written by noted authors and illustrated in full color, these are books that children really and truly *want* to read—books to excite their imagination, tickle their funny bone, expand their interests, and support their feelings. With three different reading levels, All Aboard Reading lets you choose which books are most appropriate for your children and their growing abilities.

Level 1—for Preschool through First Grade Children
Level 1 books have very few lines per page, very large type, easy words, lots of repetition, and pictures with visual "cues" to help children figure out the words on the page.

Level 2—for First Grade to Third Grade Children
Level 2 books are printed in slightly smaller type than Level 1 books. The stories are more complex, but there is still lots of repetition in the text and many pictures. The sentences are quite simple and are broken up into short lines to make reading easier.

Level 3—for Second Grade through Third Grade Children
Level 3 books have considerably longer texts, use harder words and more complicated sentences.

All Aboard for happy reading!

To Tom and Kathy Brennan's sweet bunch—
Matthew, Mark, and Kaitlin
—P. D.

To my nieces and nephews—J.D.

Special thanks to Paul L. Sieswerda, Curator, Aquarium for Wildlife
Conservation, New York.

Text copyright © 1995 by Patricia Demuth. Illustrations copyright © 1995 by Jim Deal. All
rights reserved. Published by Grosset & Dunlap, Inc., which is a member of The Putnam &
Grosset Group, New York. ALL ABOARD READING is a trademark of The Putnam & Grosset
Group. GROSSET & DUNLAP is a trademark of Grosset & Dunlap, Inc. Published
simultaneously in Canada. Printed in the U.S.A.

Library of Congress Cataloging-in-Publication Data

Demuth, Patricia.
    Way down deep / by Patricia Demuth ; illustrated by Jim Deal.
        p.   cm. — (All aboard reading)
    "Level 2, grades 1-3."
    1. Oceanography—Juvenile literature. [1. Oceanography.] I. Deal, Jim, 1956-   ill.
II. Title. III. Series.
GC21.5.D46   1995
551.46—dc20   94-39040
                                                                     CIP
ISBN 0-448-40852-X (GB)   A B C D E F G H I J   AC

ISBN 0-448-40851-1 (pbk.)   A B C D E F G H I J

ALL
ABOARD
READING™
Level 2
Grades 1-3

Way Down Deep

Strange Ocean Creatures

By Patricia Demuth
Illustrated by Jim Deal

Grosset & Dunlap • New York

Long, long ago,
explorers first sailed
across the Atlantic Ocean.

The trip was scary.

There were tales

of strange monsters—

mermaids, serpents,

and sea dragons that could

snap a ship in two.

Of course, there were no monsters.

But the ocean is full of strange creatures.

Today explorers go down,

down,

down,

into the deepest parts of the sea.

What they find is more amazing

than any of the old tales.

The ocean bottom is like another world.

In some places it is flat for miles.

In other places there are steep mountains.

Sometimes the mountaintops

rise out of the water.

These are islands.

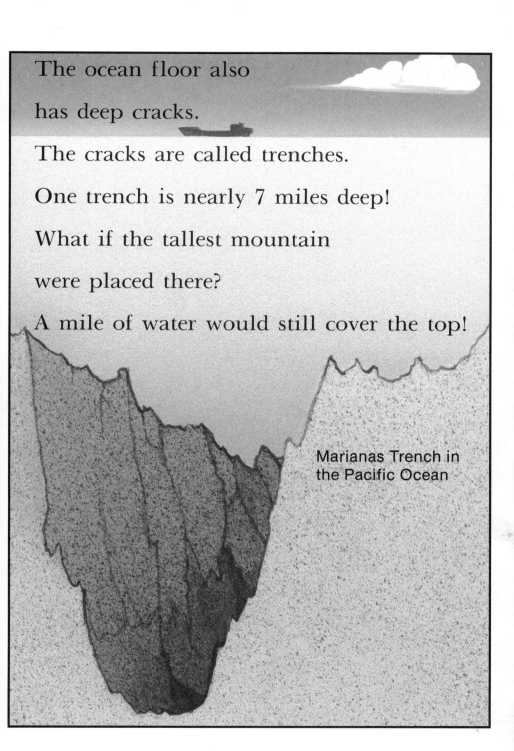

The ocean floor also
has deep cracks.
The cracks are called trenches.
One trench is nearly 7 miles deep!
What if the tallest mountain
were placed there?
A mile of water would still cover the top!

Marianas Trench in
the Pacific Ocean

We think of the ocean as blue.

But the water is only blue

and bright at the top.

That's because sunlight

shines down into it.

Farther down, the water gets darker.

Sunlight fades away.

It is too dark for plants to grow.

Finally, way down deep,

there is no light at all.

The ocean is black there.

It is cold, too—icy cold.

That's because the deep, deep waters

get almost no heat from the sun.

How do we know what it is like
in the deep ocean?
Even in special suits,
divers can't go down very far.
So scientists must find other ways.

They use little underwater boats.

They are called <u>submersibles</u>.

(You say it like this: sub-MER-si-bulls.)

Ships carry submersibles out to sea.

Then they are put overboard.

This is a famous submersible
named Alvin.

Alvin can carry three people.

It has lots of tools to do many jobs.

A floodlight lights up the dark sea.

Cameras take pictures.

A steel claw picks up things
from the ocean floor.

A probe takes the temperature
of the water.

A "vacuum cleaner" collects
sea creatures.

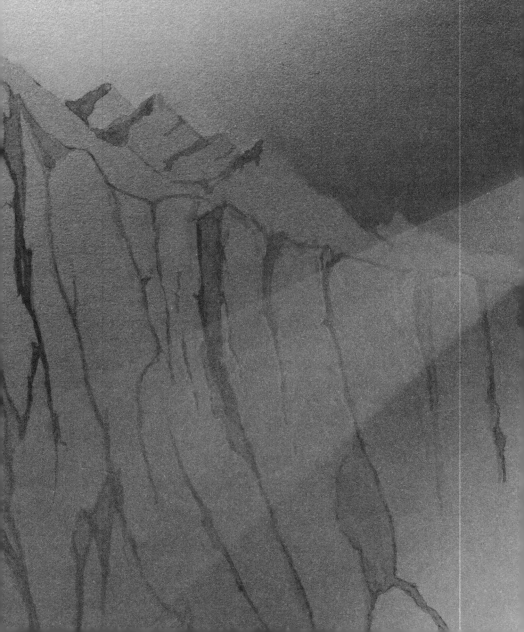

Alvin can dive down 14,000 feet.

Scientists use robots

to explore deeper water.

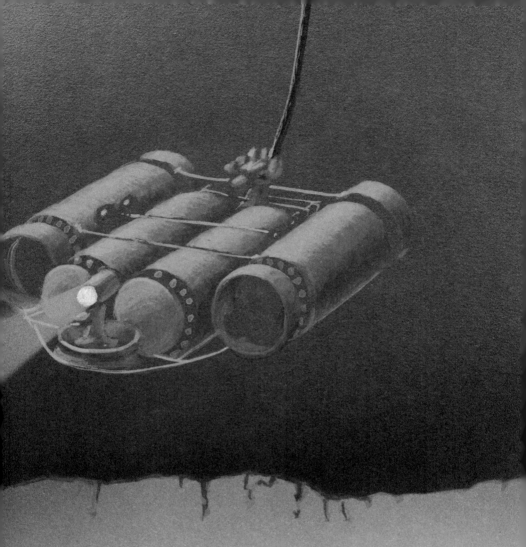

Robots can go where people cannot.

They can even go into

the deepest trenches.

The pictures they take show

what these places are like.

All these creatures live

in the deep sea.

You can see that many have

huge mouths and sharp teeth.

Food is hard to find in the dark.

When a meal passes by,

the fish are ready to grab it.

Many deepwater fish have lights
on their bodies.
Lights help fish find their mates
in the dark.
They also help fish to get food.

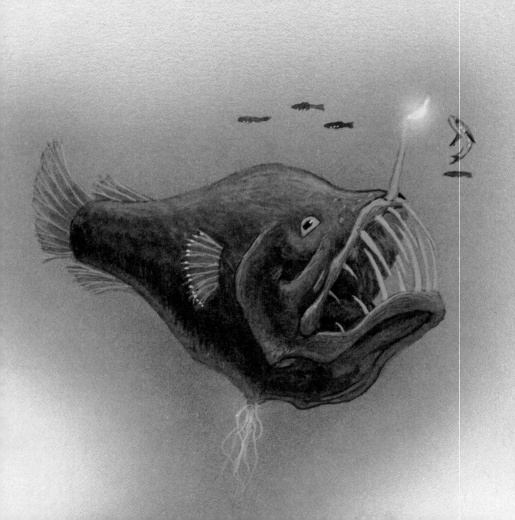

This is a deep-sea angler.

A light dangles from the top

of its head.

It looks like bait at the end

of a fishing rod.

A fish swims by.

It thinks the light is a bit of food.

GULP! The angler has dinner.

The gulper eel has a red light

at the end of its tail.

The vampire squid looks like
it wears a black cape.
Its red eyes glow in the dark.

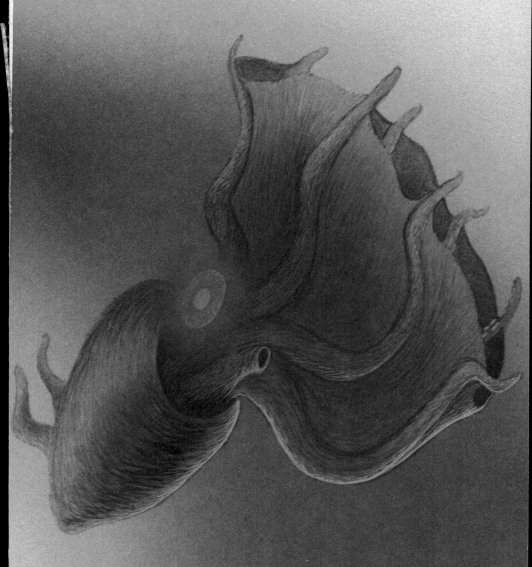

The biggest deep-sea animal of all
is the giant squid.
It can grow more than 60 feet long!
Its huge green eyes are bigger
than a man's fist.

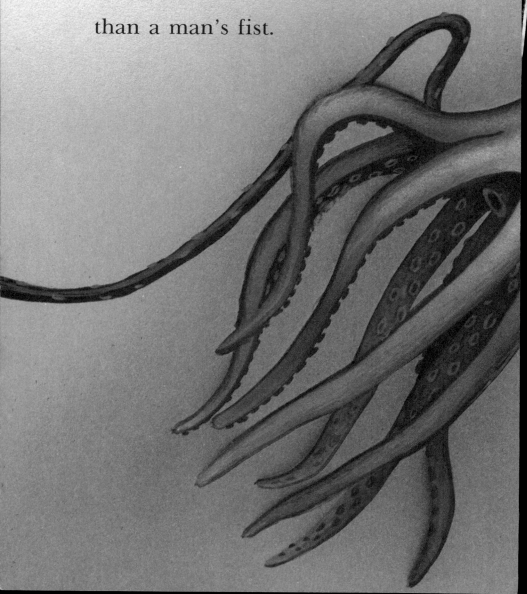

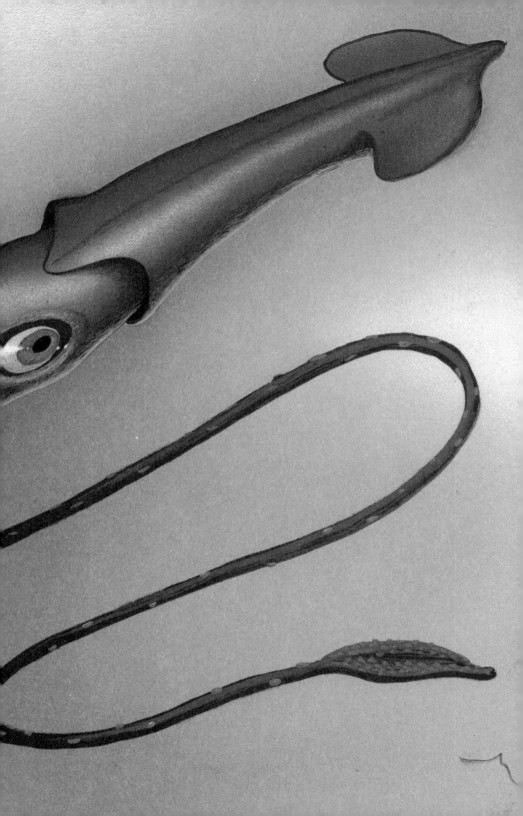

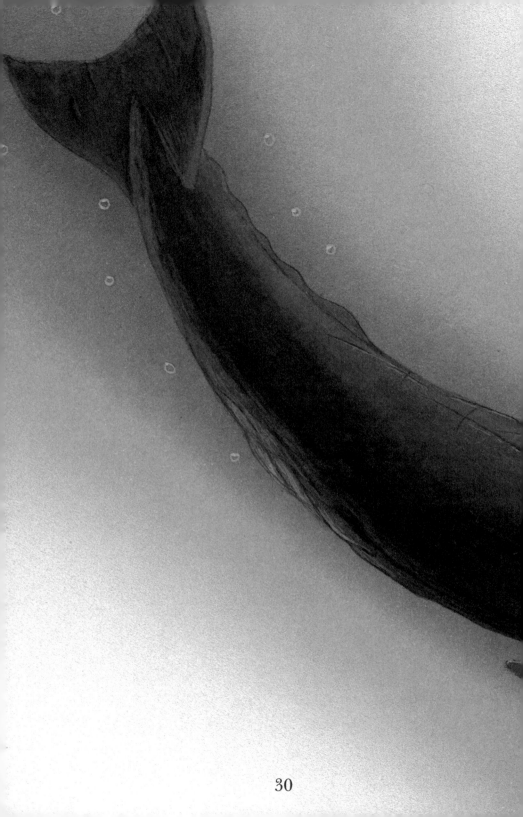

Sperm whales don't live in the deep sea.

But they are deep divers.

They come down to hunt

the giant squid.

A battle breaks out.

The giant squid wraps

its long arms and tentacles

around the sperm whale.

Its suckers cut into the whale.

Then the squid gets away.

Many animals make their home
right on the ocean floor.
Sea slugs creep about
on one small foot.

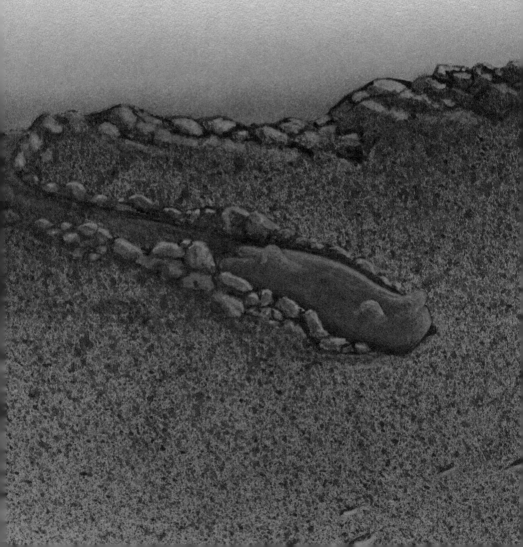

Tripod fish walk along the bottom.

They look like they have three legs.

But really the legs are fins.

These animals leave tracks

on the ocean floor—

just like animals do on land.

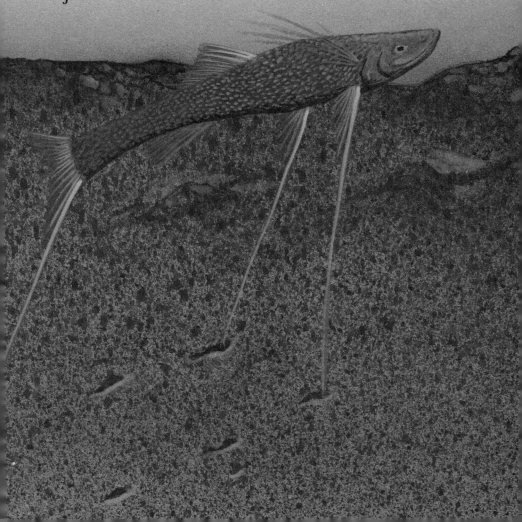

This sea cucumber sucks up mud
like a vacuum cleaner sucks up dirt.
There is a lot of good food in the mud.

Sometimes currents
stir up the mud.
Then there's a mud storm!
Bits of food fly everywhere.
The animals have a feast!

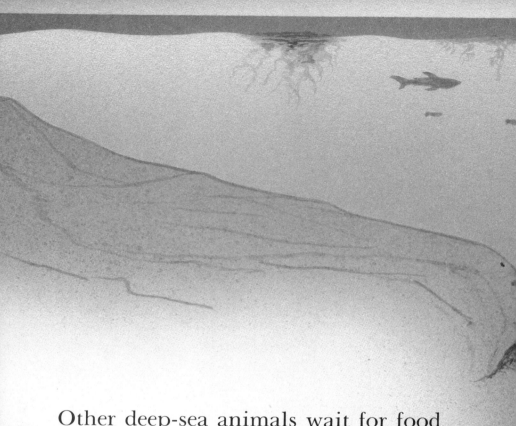

Other deep-sea animals wait for food
to fall down from above.
A rain of food is always falling
in the sea.
It comes from dead animals.
The food sinks down, down, down
to the icy-cold bottom.

Dark and cold—

that's what most

of the ocean bottom is like.

But there are hot spots, too.

Here the water is boiling hot.

How can that be?

At some places,

the ocean bottom is heated

by hot melted rocks called lava.

Lava comes from deep inside the earth.

It pushes through cracks

in the ocean bottom.

The lava heats the seawater,

just like a stove burner heats

water in a teapot.

The water can heat up to 700 degrees!

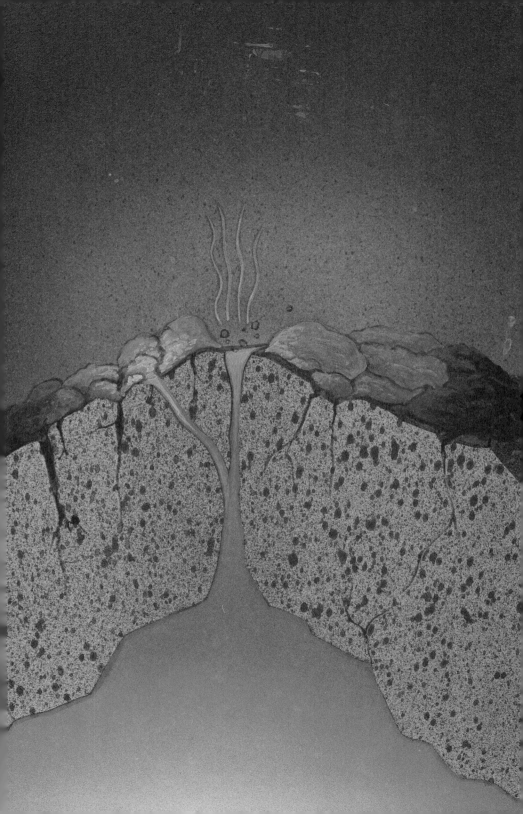

Sometimes minerals in the hot water form large chimneys.
These chimneys can be as high as a two-story house!

The water gushing out of the chimneys
is as black as smoke.
It is a strange sight to see
a row of smoking chimneys
on the ocean floor!

A zoo of odd creatures live here.
Giant worms cling to the chimneys.
Some have bright-red tips that reach
out from white cases.

On the rocks near the chimneys
are spider crabs.

They are as big as dinner plates.

Huge clams also settle near

the super-hot water.

Rich metals can be found here, too—

gold, silver, and copper.

Right now it is too hard

to dig them out.

But maybe one day we will

mine the ocean bottom.

Exploring the deep sea is like

a big treasure hunt.

Scientists discover new things every day

about the huge, watery world

way down deep!